CHANNELLED MEDITATIONS

To improve your life and the planet

By
LINDA M. BLACKSHAW

To order additional copies of this book, contact:
Xlibris
AU TFN: 1 800 844 927 (Toll Free inside Australia)
AU Local: 0283 108 187 (+61 2 8310 8187 from outside Australia)
www.xlibris.com.au
Orders@Xlibris.com.au

ISBN: Softcover   978-1-4990-0029-0
         EBook   978-1-4990-0028-3

Print information available on the last page

Rev. date: 09/30/2020

For my children Kevin, Tracy and Karen

Your dad and I are so proud of you.

Acknowledgements

Special thanks to Pat Fletcher, Sue Clennell and Jan Napier for their input on the meditations.

Very helpful, acted on some suggestions the rest stayed the same.

To Cushla Lovejoy for reading and being my trial meditator, you rock.

To Lida Parker of Melbourne your workshops and friendship have been great motivators.

Thank you.

Index of Meditations

What is Meditation?

There is no definitive answer to this, since meditation is a unique experience. Each of us connects to the universe in our own way. For some that connection is linked to God, Goddess, Divinity, Jesus, Kwan Yin, Source, Universe, Spirit or Higher Consciousness. Others connect to a space within the self; a quiet space away from the cares and stresses of daily life.

There are many ways to meditate. There is centered prayer, which can be done in silence or with a mantra (e.g. OM) repeated in the mind or spoken out loud. Gregorian chants, yoga, dancing to music, gardening, fishing or playing golf are some other forms of meditation.

Meditation can also be used in a structured way to help focus on specific ideas or outcomes. For example by taking a specific problem into a meditative state a person can sometimes get a different insight into it. This can help to resolve the problem or show a different path to take.

The meditations in this book use visualization and imagery, with specific goals in mind. By using the power of our minds we can change ourselves into more confident, stress free human beings. We can use the mind to help heal the self, rather than relying solely on outside agencies. Meditation is **not** an alternative but an addition to more conventional medicine. We can become partners in our health not just bystanders.

It is not enough to work solely on healing the self. We are all connected, one to each other and to all things. The Earth is our Mother. Our Father is the Sky. The Moon is our Sister and the Sun, our Brother. Welcome your relations. Honor and nourish them as you reconnect with your family.

What connects us?

Energy: everything and everyone are made up of energy. Rub your palms together vigorously. Palms facing each other, hold them a few centimeters apart. You can feel the energy that lies between them. Some of you may even be lucky enough to see the energy. Let's do something constructive with this energy.

Close your eyes and picture planet earth in front of you. Now, see your hands surrounding the planet and send healing energy towards earth. Now visualise healing and love soaking into the planet.

In these days of global warming, with the threats of ecological disasters as well as the effects of war, the planet is struggling. Some of the meditations in this book are a means for us all to be a part of the solution in supporting Mother Earth. To improve the quality of the air we breathe and improving the planet we live on.

Connecting Meditation

Sit with feet flat on the floor or lie down (don't lie down if you are in the habit of falling asleep while meditating) Nothing should be crossed. Lay hands on lap, palms facing up or beside you if you have chosen to lie down. Close your eyes. Focus on your breathing. Gently breathe in and out. Feel your, arms, head, legs and body, and feel the energy as it moves through your body. See it circulate around your body in a continuous spiral. Remember you are more than a body but have an aura that surrounds you as well. Notice the energy field is wider than the physical. As the energy surrounds you, it pulses brightly growing stronger and stronger. With each beat it grows wider and reaches out to touch everything around you, furniture, walls and out beyond into the universe. You are a giant pulsing ball of energy. The sun and moon nourish you. See yourself reaching out and touching clouds and stars. Feel the connection that you have with all things. The energy is the same. It just takes different forms.

Sometimes after a 'Connecting' meditation you can still feel your connection to other things hours later.

After one such meditation, I was walking down to the shops. I stopped and stared at the blue sky and large white clouds. A feeling of great joy pulsed through me and I felt I could just reach out and touch the clouds. Now, years later I can still reconnect with the joy of being one with the clouds.

As in any book the meditations all can be used as is BUT you can add, subtract and create your own. Do a different meditation each day by following the set order or dive in wherever you like. Beginning with the self-healing then sending love and energy to others and to the planet can help to instigate change. We already understand that the alcoholic or addict can only change themselves when they are ready to do so. Yet, by making a change within ourselves and in our attitude to their disease we can also effect change in them.

Therefore what **I** do in my life and in my part of the world can eventually impact somewhere else. It may take some time but it will happen.

Each small step can build to a tidal wave. Let us take that step. If we start to think about it we can get overwhelmed or place it in the too hard basket or procrastinate or postpone it and never start.

STOP

LET'S START
NOW

Create the Life, Health and Love you want for yourself, then extend it outwards. Be the pebble that is tossed into the pond that creates the ripples that radiate outwards from the core.

We are the core.

We are the heart.

We are the planet.

We are one.

Let that be our mantra. Let those fifteen words be the basis of our philosophy. Let Love and Respect be our guides, not hate or harm. Cherish self and differences. Respect self and differences. This does not mean we will like or always agree with everyone. Life would be boring if we all agreed! It does mean that we can become less judgmental of others.

I prefer to work in a circle however you may wish to visualize a pyramid, a pentagram, a tepee or any geometric shape. Work with whatever you want, with what **you** are most comfortable. In any meditation **relax and just be**.

The words are just a guide. Sometimes in a guided meditation the instructions are to imagine you are walking in a rose garden. Your reaction is not to do that and you find yourself walking on a beach or up a mountain. Go with what you are feeling and seeing. **Intent is the key**, not the how or the where. It matters **not** how you make the connection but that you **do**.

***

I remember at a crystal bowl meditation evening of sound healing. The facilitator (I prefer this to leader as it is easier to do own thing with the instructions. A leader implies that we have to follow blindly.) said, " Reconnect to the tones. Let your sounds out."

Now I have difficulty with even going "OM" out loud in a room by myself never mind in a room full of people. But I thought, okay, I would do it. I WILL DO IT.

I could feel tension rising up. I closed my eyes and tried to reconnect with my sound. It was amazing. I did not find sound but found something more precious. I was bathed in a golden light as I sat beside a waterfall. There were animals by my feet, at the top of the waterfall and in a pool. In that moment I realized that, that evening I couldn't reconnect with tones but I did connect with spirit or totem animals.

I did not hear another word or sound until we were recalled back to the room when the meditation was brought to a close. I felt terrific. This experience reinforced the instruction to relax and go where you are taken and not to follow the spoken instruction blindly unless that's where you are meant to go. Remember: meditation is about relaxing and going with the flow. Follow your intuition.

In alternative medicine and also in traditional there is an emphasis on being balanced. We can all recall advertisements that exhort us to put our lives in balance. Some of the meditations in this book talk about putting yourself in balance by working on seven energy centres or chakras.

Each chakra has a specific purpose and if blocked can impact negatively on our lives as follows:

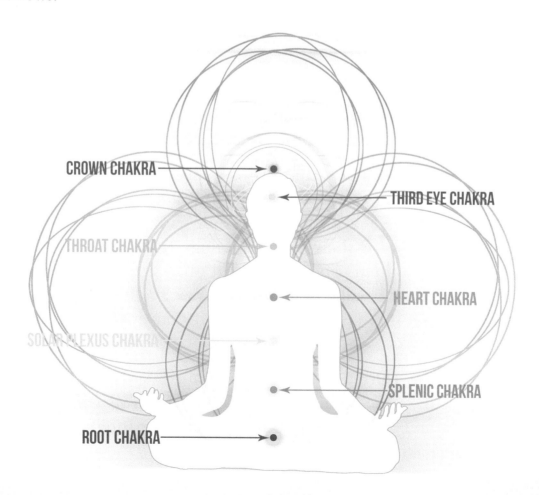

1. **The Root or Base Chakra** can also be called Muladhara is concerned with survival (the flight or fight response), physical identity. It is a grounding point of the Spirit in the body at birth. A blockage here can affect stamina and basic stability, possible bowel problems, irrational anger or paralyzing fear. Often shown as the colour red.

2. **The Sacral Chakra** also called Svadhisthana is located in the lower abdomen around the reproductive system in females and the genitals in males. This center helps us explore our needs and desires initially through the five senses. In this chakra we can work to rekindle self-love and self-worth. If blocked can dull intuition. Also addictive behavior may affect this chakra. Orange is the colour for this area.

3. **The Solar Plexus** or Manipura is located above the navel and includes the stomach and sometimes lungs. Its function is related to your personal power. Conscious thought and rationalization are its concerns. A blockage here can be linked to anxiety, mood swings, anger and negative feelings and impede the ability to make choices. The colour yellow is connected to the solar plexus. Intuition is impacted if there is a blockage here. The phrase "gut feeling" is based in the truth.

4. **The Heart Chakra** or Anahata is located in the center of this chest over heart, lungs and breasts. Its energy also covers hands and arms. This chakra is seen as the seat of the soul and is linked to harmony, peace and love. Green or pink are the colours for this chakra.

5. **The Throat Chakra** or Vishuddha is located at the front of the neck and a blockage here can cause sore throats, swollen neck glands, mouth ulcers and ear problems. People with a blockage here have difficulty in sharing their deeper feelings with themselves and with those close to them. They are closed off. Even people who talk a lot can have a blockage here and when we really listen to them we can hear that there is no depth to their conversations. Blue is the colour here.

6. **The Brow or Third Eye Chakra** also called Ajna is just above the bridge of the nose in the center of the brow. It is concerned with eyes, ears and both hemispheres of the brain. Indigo is associated with this chakra.

7. **The Crown Chakra** or Sahasrara is located at the top of the head in the center; some systems show this chakra as being just above the body rather than on it. This is the chakra most closely connected to Spirit and the merging of all three levels of the body, physical, emotional and spiritual. It is about being rather than acting.
Some books show violet in connection with the Crown others white or even gold.

You can work on the chakras individually or as a whole, with colour I combine balancing the chakras with Reiki, a form of energy healing and to assist in this I use a stone called a Shiva Lingam. This stone helps to bring all the chakras into balance. In a Reiki session, my client holds the stone in their left hand being closest to the Heart Chakra. The creation of a balanced flow of energy through the body and the chakra system is assisted by the use of this stone. Sometimes it is difficult to automatically remember which colour relates to which chakra and I suggest you see a spinning rainbow circle over each chakra and imagine the chakra taking the coloured energy it needs.

Affirmations are an important aid in healing the body, improving the self and in reprogramming our thinking. It is vital in using affirmations to use the present tense, to be the result e.g. if you are dieting you could use **I am taller and thinner and people notice me** or if you have a desired weight you would say **I am now 60 kilos.**

Also become aware of your self talk as we can sabotage the positive by placing in subtle negatives. Avoid but at all costs. I can now stop the thought when I hear but or doubt creeping in. Become Mindful in your thinking.

Going into your Sacred Space can be a starting point for the meditations in this book. There is no hard and fast rule. Do what is right for you. Some of you will wish to follow the order and some of you will just want to rush in. Others may find that they keep repeating a particular meditation or can do all except for one. That is fine. However, if you keep avoiding a particular meditation or one makes you feel uncomfortable, look within. A meditation that you always liked can suddenly make you uncomfortable. Look to your own life. Ask questions. Is there something that makes me uncomfortable? Is there something going on around me which I am missing? Is there something that I wish to avoid confronting in my life?

Sometimes when we need to work on the throat chakra we will avoid working in that area. Try a chakra meditation. Close your eyes and scan your body. Does a particular chakra feel blocked or look dull? Is there a chakra that makes you really uncomfortable? Go into a meditative state and ask why?

If you still cannot figure this out on your own take the problem into your Sacred Space. Invite in a Guide or Guides (sometimes it is a good idea to call in male and female to get different perspectives) and ask for their help. Take note of what you feel and what you see and hear.

Creating a Sacred Space (i)

Close your eyes and imagine your favorite flower. Breathe in and out. Fill your abdomen and with each out breath watch as the petals peel back slowly. Move in closer and begin to sink deeper and deeper into the heart of the flower. As you draw closer to the center, you see a door. Open it and walk through. You find yourself in a room. This is your special place, which is for you and you alone. Only those you invite may enter here. In the middle of your room is a comfortable day bed. On this bed you can connect with Spirit, receive healing or just relax.

Lie down on the bed. Feel the healing energy moving through the top of your head and down your body to your toes. As it moves through and over your body any dark bits of negativity and disease are removed. As the energy moves through your body it revitalizes and energises everything in its path. Body, mind and spirit begin to throb with a clear pulsing energy, that refreshes everything it touches.

On your body you see spinning discs which are on your energy centres or chakras. Energy is flooding through you, cleansing the chakras and activating all your talents. Beginning at the top of your head the energy begins to move creating a figure of eight, with the cross over point the middle of your body. At first the movement is slow then gathers speed and becomes a blur. This eternal energy heals as it passes over your body.

Move into a specific meditation here or just relax in the healthy energy.

When it is time to leave your Sacred Space or meditation know that the healing energy still flows through you. Stand up, wriggle your toes and connect with the Earth to ground yourself. As you leave it for the everyday world see your body and auric field encased in a pure white light shell which will repel any negativity. Only those things you need to experience will get through. The white light shell also protects your energy from other people.

Creating a Sacred Space (ii)

Close your eyes and see yourself walking along a riverbank. The water is calm in places, gentle lapping waves in others, and tumbling over rocks creating rapids falling away over steep rocks to form large waterfalls. You can hear the water as well as birds and other animals. As you walk you see a bridge. You are eager to cross this bridge. This bridge takes you to your special place. It might be somewhere you love to visit or a place from your imagination. It may be on another planet, under the sea, inside or out. This is your place, so create whatever you want. In your space you see a day bed. On this bed you can connect with your Guides, receive healing or just relax and de-stress.

As you lie down you feel energy begin to move. It comes in through the top of your head and moves down through your body, removing any bits of negativity or disease that it finds. It carries the rubbish out through your toes and disperses it into the earth. The energy continues to move, refreshing everything it touches. Mind, body and spirit all begin to pulse with a clean pure energy.

On your body you see spinning discs. They are placed over your chakras. Energy is flooding through you, cleansing and refreshing your physical body, your aura and your soul. The energy is also activating all your talents, allowing you to achieve the highest possible for yourself. The energy is removing the limits you place on yourself. The energy pulses through you in an eternal figure of eight.

You can now move into another meditation or just enjoy the being in the energy.

When it is time to return to the present, close this meditation as described in Creating Sacred Space (i).

The following meditations can be done on their own or as part of a Sacred Space meditation. It is important to be relaxed before you begin so a simple breathing and relaxing technique should be done if you choose not to go into your sacred Space.

Eagle energy is connected to philosophy and ideals. In this instance eagle is concerned with clear seeing and making a connection with Earth and Sky.

Eagle

Invite Eagle into your Sacred Space. Watch as eagle swoops down and lands in front of you. Look into his amber eyes. As you look, you feel yourself begin to sink into the eagle. Your feet are now claws, feel them flex in the earth.

Shrug your shoulders and feel your muscles ripple. Look down and admire your feathers. You and the eagle are one. Feel the power surge through you as you spread your wings. You begin to run, flap your wings and aim for the sky. As you soar, you realize your eyesight has become keener. You pass over and through clouds and as you look below you can see your Sacred Space. What does it look like? On thermal currents, hover, look beyond your personal space and look at the planet. As you fly over it you see the earth's aura. It is muddy and heavy.

Feel the eagle energy fire out through his/your eyes. This energy floods the Earth's aura. See the Earth's aura become a pulsing stream of pure clear energy. See the grey negative aura being blasted away and as it settles the planet is now surrounded by particles of positive energy. The earth is glowing and pulsing with freedom.

As Eagle turns back towards your sacred Space you hover above it. You see yourself from the Eagle's perspective. Look down and see yourself and your aura. What does your aura look like? There are many colours in your auric field but some are bright, some are cloudy and some are hidden behind clouds of black negativity. Your eagle's eyes become sharper and pure white energy charges from them and into your auric field. It blasts through the black negative ions and replaces them with pulsing positive energy. As the black and gray negativity vanishes, the white energy enriches and brightens all the colours that surround you. The eagle energy reinforces your protective armour. Eagle swoops into your Sacred Space once more and lands beside your body. His beak touches your chest and you slip back into your body.

You feel full of healthy energy. You are happy and confident, comfortable in your own skin.

I am happy. I am confident. I focus on my Goals.

I AM PROUD TO BE ME

Badger stands for assertiveness and protection in conflict.

Mouse represents vulnerability and elusiveness and also getting out of tight corners.

Coyote is known as the trickster but also protection in sticky situations

The Salamanders in this meditation are fire sprites

Badger, Mouse, Coyote and Salamander

Picture yourself sitting in a green meadow surrounded by trees. Beside you there is a patch of soil. It is rich and dark. As you sit, a mouse comes scurrying up. It is curious and shows no fear. Badger approaches and bares its teeth. Yet you sense that its ferocious nature will not harm you. Now you notice a salamander (a fire sprite), lazing in the sun. As the sun sets the salamander raises its head and along with mouse and badger gazes at you: all seem to be waiting for something or someone. A coyote slips through the trees.

The mouse gives a tug at your toe and mouse, badger and salamander lead you to a hollow. As you draw closer to it the hollow, it opens up and a path appears. Coyote follows behind; he is guarding your back. You follow badger, mouse and salamander into the earth while Coyote remains at the opening. They lead you down into a large crystal cavern. You know this is the core, the heart of the planet.

Some of the crystals are bright and pulse strongly; some of the crystals are dark and still and some of the crystals are dim and flutter.

The heart of the Earth has an irregular beat. You cry and your tears fall on the floor of the crystal. Tears of compassion and love. Tears that cleanse and purify. You cry for the Earth and you cry for yourself. As the tears fall you feel your heart ease. As your tears fall you feel the earth ease.

You connect with Universal Energy. Feel the power grow in the palms of your hands, soles of your feet and in your heart chakra. Continuous streams of healing energy pour out of your body. Mouse, Badger and Salamander catch the energy, jump on the energy and ride on it. They run back and forth helping you take the energy to the dead and dying crystals.

The Earth Mother welcomes your tears, welcomes the healing energy. She breathes in your love. You watch the healing energy flow from the Universe through you to Badger, Mouse and Salamander and through the crystals. This energy follows a continuous arc. When all the crystals are beating strongly you call for Coyote, who comes running. He bathes in the Universal energy.

You hold your palms together and bow your head in respect and to thank the Universe. The arc stops moving and the energy slowly is absorbed by Badger, Mouse, Salamander and Coyote and yourself. All of you move out of the cave, along the path back to the moonlit meadow. You thank Badger, Mouse, Salamander and Coyote for their help.

Badger reminds you to call on his energy at anytime, whenever you struggle to assert yourself. They vanish into the night. You sit for a few minutes and repeat

I PROTECT MYSELF.

I ASSERT MYSELF.

I ACCEPT MYSELF.

Anytime you need to be reminded and connect to Badger and Coyote for assistance repeat the affirmations as you call on the animals to be present. When you feel ready, return to the present. Take a few deep breaths, stretch into your body then open your eyes.

Bear energy is healing and also to do with introspection and strength.

Bear Energy

Invite Bear to join you in your Sacred Space. See the Grizzly, the Brown, the Black all kinds of bears. They stand tall, with their hind paws planted in the Earth. Feel their strength, feel their power ebb and flow in a continuous loop.

What cares and troubles do you have? What negative thoughts do you have about yourself? Hand them over to the bears. They have strong shoulders.

See the bears eat your problems. See your cares, negative thoughts and emotions pass to the bears. See the bears swallow and absorb them. Now hear the bears growling. They growl out your pain. With each growl, you feel lighter. Feel your emotions ease. You are no longer weighted down by ill health and repressed emotions. Negative thought patterns are no more. Your spirit is growing lighter and you feel the seeds of self love begin to grow. You stand tall in the Cave of the Bear. Open your eyes, mind and heart. What message does Bear have for you? Listen to the Bear's song. Let the healing power of Bear energy work its magic.

Now, picture the Earth and visualize the Mother's pain. See drought stricken areas, see war torn countries and see fish struggling to breathe. See the Mother's tears feel her pain. Feel her sorrow. Picture many Bears and ask the Mother to pass her cares, all her woes and all her anguished tears over to them. See all of them being removed. See the bears swallow her woes and tears. Hear them growl out the Mother's pain. See the growled out pain transform into healing rain and healing energy. Watch as Mother Earth is showered with positive blessings.

See Peace. See Love.

Respect the Planet. Respect Ourselves

Buffalo is wisdom, practicality, abundance and prayer.

Wolf is about teaching leadership and family dynamics.

Owl is about sacred knowledge and spiritual wisdom.

Buffalo, Wolf and Owl

Visualize yourself walking on the Earth in your bare feet. As you walk, pause every so often; clench and unclench your toes. As you wriggle your toes, connect to the Earth, feel sand, feel soil and feel grass. Sunset showers orange on the scene and the night softens to pale yellow fading into blue grey.

As you walk notice that you are moving amongst buffalo. Feel their strength. You see a White Buffalo and slowly move towards it. The White buffalo stands and waits for you. The buffalo raises its head proudly and you look into his dark eyes. Dark eyes full of compassion and understanding. You place your hands in his rough wool neck ruff and close your fist within it. As you listen, the bellows of the buffalo mingle with the howls of the wolf and the hoots of owls. The howls and hoots come from a mountain.

The buffalo begins to move and walks you towards the sounds. He leads you to the foot of the mountain where you see some wolves. The wolves stop howling and one wolf comes towards you. He gently takes your free hand and tugs. You follow and sense the wolves wish you to sit on the ground amongst them. Their eyes glow in the moonlight. As you sit you open your heart to the message the wolves are sending you. You open up to the wisdom that is flowing to you and you connect to Earth. You become one with the grass and soil, one with the mountain and one with all things of Nature.

The hoots of the owl call on your Spirit to expand, to connect with the Akashic Records: an information repository which holds all knowledge of human lives (past, present and future) and of the Universe. Share your compassion, your love and your energy with the wolves, owls and buffaloes. Visualize the wolves, owls and buffaloes moving off to the different corners of the Earth. Remember to share the love and compassion with yourself. We are all a part of the equation that is Life.

Reconnecting With Spirit

If you are doing these meditations as part of a circle, Medicine Wheel or Pyramid, they are done in the middle. The meditation can be done with a crystal in your hand. My choice would be either amethyst or smokey quartz or perhaps amber for its protective qualities. Rose quartz is also good as it represents love. Any crystal you are drawn to works. The crystal can be real or imagined.

The aim is to reconnect with your Soul which dwells within for we are Souls with a physical body not physical beings whose soul is held somewhere separate.

LOTUS

Keeping your breathing even, visualise an opening in your heart centre. Make yourself small and enter your heart. There is a small light. It looks like the small bud of a flower. There is tingling beneath your feet and at the top of your head. You open up a channel and Universal Light Energy moves through your body. As the Universal Light Energy moves through your Heart Centre the bud slowly unfurls, petals open up, and the lotus reveals itself to you. Your soul expands and spreads out from your body. Feel the Universal Light radiate through your being. Your body, aura and soul resonate with Light. Your soul has expanded.

(This can also be a moving meditation.)

Crouch down and cover your head with your arms. Slowly unwind your arms from around your head. Straighten your back and slowly get to your feet. Stretch your body and widen your arms and spread your fingers wide. You are trying to reach the sky. As you connect with Universal energy feel your body begin to tingle and feel the Universal Energy flow through you. Feel your soul reach out to reconnect with the Universe.

Hedgehog is about protection especially self protection, adaptability, sensitivity to nature rhythms and defensiveness. Hedgehog has also been described as the Shield of The Soul

Hedgehog

See your Soul as a young hedgehog. Your Soul is soft and needs nurturing. Imagine the gentle healing energy of Rose quartz surrounding you. Breathe in the color Rose. As you exhale breathe out any dark negative emotions, low self-esteem and any hateful thoughts that you have. Any dark patches in your physical and auric body become dimmer then vanish. As you inhale visualize positivity and love filling you. With each inhalation you feel your body tingle and vibrate as it fills with love, with positive emotions. With each breath you are gaining in confidence and self-worth. Eventually you are breathing out as much love as you breathe in.

Now, your aura is filled with positive vibrations. Visualize your soul- the young hedgehog -swell and grow.

With love and knowledge your soul is armoured and like the adult hedgehog you can prick and deflect those who attack.

An affirmation: **My Soul is Strong.**

My Soul is Love.

I am Strong.

I am Love

Unicorn: Healing Earth

Imagine you are in the center of the Earth. You are at its Heart. You can visualize this as anything you wish; perhaps you are in a crystal cave. Wherever you choose to be there will be a giant lake.

All toxins are gathered there. It has become a liquid time bomb. You hear it ticking. Each tick brings an explosion closer.

The damage from Acid Rain, Global Warming and manufactured poisons are all gathering here. Now see people depositing their racial and religious hate, their distrust, violence, black depression, droughts, disease and famine into the toxic pool. Anything that demeans and lessens humanity: anything that affects the human condition in a negative manner is deposited in this pool.

Visualize Unicorns coming from all corners of the Universe. The Unicorns are a brilliant white with long spiral horns. They march in line towards the pool and each dips their horn into the putrid poison. With each dipping of the Unicorns' horns all the toxins are slowly removed.

Once the lake is clean and sparkling the Unicorns march away. A stairway leading up to the sky appears. Source is waiting to clear away the toxins, returning the horns to a pristine state.

See the earth and its people becoming new born. The Unicorn brings rebirth, the return of Enchantment. See things through a child's eye. The World is an amazing place. Bring back wonder into your life. Return to Innocence. Begin a new page and create balance of SoulHeartMind. All is reborn.

**

Further suggestions with this meditation:

Connect with Robin Redbreast energy, which stands for purity and compassion, sharing hardship, courage, friendship, loyalty and protection.

Connect with otter who is playful and a child of joy.

Both these animals can be incorporated either separately or together as a conclusion to the Unicorn meditation. They can also be included within the meditation as can any other animals that appear whilst you are in a meditative state.

Improve Self-Esteem and Self-Confidence

The animals I was given to work with on improving self-esteem and self-confidence will, at first glance seem quite disparate. However, they have similar and complimentary correspondences. Initially, you may feel it is easier to focus on each animal individually. That is fine. Remember if other animals fit in with your belief system you can include or replace any of them, whatever makes you comfortable.

Moose: build self-esteem, know when to talk and when to be silent, learn to give self a pat on the back for anything done well, empowerment, brings true self-confidence, helps us leave the past behind so we can move confidently into the future. Moose is about shared joy.

Skunk: will power, helps to get rid of the people who hold us back, the people who feed our lack of belief in ourselves, gives us permission to grow, projects self respect and helps us become comfortable in our own skin. Skunk is about reputation and respect.

Crow: walk your talk, walk in beauty, stand tall and strut your stuff, personal integrity, allows us to reach full potential, to find our own distinctive voice.

By invoking the energies of Moose, Skunk and Crow we will learn to assert ourselves and stand our ground. We will be able to trust that we will know when it is time to fight or time to walk away.

Moose, Skunk and Crow

Take deep breaths and settle yourself into your Sacred Space. Center yourself, open up your senses and connect to your true self. Explore how you see yourself. What do you feel about you? Your inner child, the seat of your self-confidence is open to you. There is no place to hide. Doubts on your abilities lie here: doubts that sabotage or lessen your confidence in your achievements and your abilities.

See the child pop out of your body. Your child looks around and spots three animals- Moose, Skunk and Crow. Crow flies and caws drawing the child to the trio. Fearful yet with the innocence and determination of childhood your child pushes forward. A hand goes out to touch the Moose. Energy pulses into the child. Moose rumbles" This energy is freely given, draw on this to leave fear behind. Grow tall in your abilities. You can achieve much. I remove your limitations. Believe in yourself- acknowledge your achievements. Feel the joy of true confidence pulse through you. Tap into this energy any time you need to assert your rights" Moose bows to the child and the energy flow shuts down. Your child still holds the moose energy within its body.

Skunk brushes against the child's legs and weaves the eternal infinity symbol. The child's eyes widen as he/she hears skunk's words inside his/her head. Energy pulses through the child. Energy pulses through your child in a figure of eight. The pulse is light at first then slowly increases its intensity." Respect yourself. You are a wonderful child of the Universe. Know that you can achieve anything. Remove limitations. It is time to remove yourself from people who feed your negativity, who feed your self-doubt. My energy will create a barrier between them and you. My energy will help you create better boundaries. Your true self is confident. It is time to reveal your true self. It is time to become comfortable with who you are. It is time to remove the bindings that restrict. To remove the negative programming from this and past lives. To remove the voice that holds us back. To remove the voice that says you can't, you won't. The voice, that stops you from even trying. It is time to be the you, you can be. Be all you can be. My energy is reputation and respect, any time you falter or feel under attack call on skunk energy. My energy will bolster your self-respect. My energy will help you feel comfortable in your own skin, to be proud of who you are and help you stand tall and confident in yourself. Skunk stands back and the child feels the energy pull back. Yet, feels it still lodged within his/her body skunk energy, lies waiting for its call to action.

Crow caws once more. The child feels a tickle in his/her throat, which grows to a warm tingle. From the crow's beak the child hears" I carry your personal integrity. It is time to talk with your true voice. You are a child of beauty. Find and connect with your true self. It is time to walk your talk, stand tall and be proud. Strive for your full potential. When you can't find the words call on me to help you reconnect with your authentic self. To remember your own distinctive voice."

From within your child a voice soars

I am confident.

I walk my path with pride.

I know when to listen.

I know when to talk.

I am comfortable being me.

I love and accept me.

The child thanks Moose, Skunk and Crow for their gifts. Your child returns to you and jumps back into your body.

You feel energy pulsing through your body in the eternal figure of eight. It shoves out your negativity and self-doubt. Moose energy empowers you. Skunk energy boosts your confidence and self esteem. Crow works on your throat chakra so you can find and use your voice.

Joy infuses you and you stay for a while in your Sacred Space enjoying this new energised you. When it is time to return to the now, you know these energies return with you to help you be the you that you can be.

I walk my talk.

I stand tall.

I am comfortable in my skin.

My voice is true.

I respect myself.

I am a child of joy.

I AM HAPPY AND LOVE BEING ME.

****

Stress

Stress is the bane of the modern age. Most of us have suffered from it, at some time in our lives. Whilst for many it is a short term or one off instance, for others it is a deep-seated emotion that controls our lives.

Some stress can be beneficial as it can cause us to react in a positive manner in certain situations. Therefore the first thing to do is to discover what is at the root of the stress. The following meditation connects to Giraffe, who is a stress free animal and can be called on for general stress. Although this is a stand-alone meditation it can be an excellent lead in to connect other animals, targeting specific problems or to improve conditions that stress exacerbates e.g. fertility problems.

If your stress is caused by financial problems call on Kangaroo or Pelican. The energies of both animals are linked to abundance. Health stress could be assisted by linking to Bear Energy, as the cave of Mother Bear is a place of healing. Bees could also be invoked, in particular their honey which is a natural antibiotic.

Giraffe

Go into your Sacred Space or close your eyes and breathe deeply. There is a large screen in front of you. It flickers to life. There are trees and grassy flat plains all over the screen. At the edge of the screen a movement draws your attention. Long legs stroll into view. A Giraffe ambles over to a tree and stops. As you watch the Giraffe stretches its neck, its tongue slips out. It rolls a leaf into its mouth and slowly chews. You admire how relaxed it is. As it begins to move you match its lope to your own. With each step you become the Giraffe. You feel giraffe energy move through your body. A gentle feeling that soothes rattled nerves; that removes tension. You straighten your spine, elongate your neck, stretch your body, rotate your shoulders, tighten and relax muscles. As you lazily stroll along, with each step your body merges with the giraffe. Once you feel calm, loose and relaxed, you thank Giraffe and return to the present. You watch Giraffe stroll away.

Surround your unstressed body in a White Light cocoon. Only those things that you need to experience will get through. Outside stresses are held at bay. Slowly come back to the present; gently stretch into your body, arms, legs, and neck then rotate your shoulders. Smile softly and ease back into the now.

Anytime you start to feel stress overwhelm you, reconnect with the Giraffe energy now held within you. As you feel the calming energy flow through you, tense and relax your muscles. Recharge your White Light, Mirror Shield or whichever protective barrier you use.

****

If temporary lack of sleep or long term insomnia is at the root of your stress, Giraffe energy is not a good idea. Giraffe's are known for their ability to endure long periods without sleep. For sleep problems, call on koala or sloth as these animals spend much time asleep or you could imagine a swan and visualise it helping you glide peacefully into sleep.

An active mind can hinder the onset of sleep and sometimes by using an affirmation can help. Repeating " My mind is still and I slip into sleep" or something similar may be beneficial.

Some other uses for Giraffe Energy

Another aspect of giraffes is connected to sight as they are noted for their ability to see long distances. One way to utilise this is to focus on the giraffe's eyes and see yourself looking through them. Draw on this energy to improve your distance vision. You could also invoke giraffe to help you look into the future and assist in moving towards your goals.

Pregnancy

As soon as you decide that you wish to fall pregnant both of you need to get started on a new health regimen. Increase your folatc level e.g. bread with higher folate content. Improve your diet, cut out smoking and if a heavy or binge drinker stop or at least cut right back.

Get some Rose Quartz and/or Red Jasper for your bedroom and carry some smaller pieces with you.

Each night before sleep (or anytime you feel like it) relax and visualise a rose pink light infusing your womb and your ovaries if you are a women and your testes if you are a man. This rose pink light will search out any negativity in the reproductive system and light it up with love. Yellow would also be a good colour connection as it is a bright happy colour. If other colours intrude, find out what they mean e.g. whilst red is good for passion it also can be seen as anger. What does it mean to you?

If you are having difficulty falling pregnant then use the Giraffe meditation to minimise the stress. Make your own fertility pouch. Herbal magick can be helpful.

If you still have no luck and have to resort to medical intervention then you can still use meditation to assist.

You may be told that there is no medical reason for your inability to fall pregnant. This may be a good time to try hypnotherapy as it can target any deep-seated fears etc. I believe both partners should have at least one session as it takes two to create a baby.

If In Vitro Fertilisation is your final stage then still use those tools already suggested plus at any medical procedure, harvesting your eggs or implanting the foetus take yourself to your Sacred Space and call on the Healing energies for assistance.

You will have noticed that apart from Giraffe I have not mentioned any animals in relation to becoming pregnant. When I researched the fertility animals I could not ignore the other meanings either spiritual or mundane. Rabbits dealt with fertility but also represented fear. Cows could bring up visions of submissiveness and docility and bulls could bring to mind dominance and aggression. Dolphins have healing energy and gentleness but they also have the capacity to be violent.

In any meditation an animal can show its face. It is up to you to decide the meaning. Don't forget to examine <u>how the animal makes you feel,</u> as this is the deciding factor to continuing to work with that animal to facilitate your pregnancy. What message has the animal brought you? Use your intuition and listen for the message.

Once you have achieved your goal don't forget to continue with the colour therapy and visualisations. Send your baby love, talk to your baby and play music for him/her.

Talk to your partner, midwife or doctor of any fears you have. Do not bottle them up. You will notice that I have omitted friends and other mums and pregnant women. For some reason their stories all come across as horrific. Ignore them, if it was that bad we'd all stop at one child (I have three!)

Remember to relax, go into your Healing Space and visualise love, peace and welcome for the coming baby. Use affirmations.

Treat yourself to a massage or even a Reiki session either before, during pregnancy and/or after. Babies love Reiki energy in the womb and after they are born. Once the baby arrives give him/her regular massages too. Most babies love it.

As a baby shower gift a voucher for the beauty salon is an excellent Mum to Be present as would a Reiki session.

Women as you try to fall pregnant and have your baby do not forget your partner. Yes, they are there to support you but this is their journey as well. Include them, acknowledge any fears they may have but **most importantly** don't exclude them. You share the developing baby not just the creation of it or the upbringing.

Creating Your Own Meditations

Sometimes everyday happenings carry messages. We may try to ignore them. However if we keep hearing particular words and sounds, seeing the same things e.g a willy wagtail, smells or have repetitive dreams we should try to discover their meanings.

Dreams are probably the easiest to work out as we can refer to a dream dictionary or already have a dream reference worked out for ourselves e.g. being stuck and unable to move may mean that there is a problem we cannot get away from.

Another way to define the dream and gain understanding of it is simply write it down, read it through, lay it aside then re-read it later. Sometimes throughout the day, you recall more of your dream, record it. Distancing yourself from the dream can be beneficial, as when you read about your dream later on, you can be more objective than when you first awoke.

Focused meditation is a good tool in dream interpretation. Go into your Sacred Space, relax and recall your dream. Imagine there is a TV screen in front of you and watch your dream unfold. Ask your Guides, Angels or Higher Self bring clarity to your dream. Explore every aspect of your dream, physical, emotional and search for any hidden meanings.

A starting point for the omens we see, hear or smell is, to find out if they stimulate a particular memory e.g. the smell lily-of-the-valley perfume reminds me my late mother. She died when I was 12 yet over fifty years later that smell still evokes my mum's memory.

Reference books or the Internet are other tools to utilise. If you keep being drawn to a particular things discover their meaning. For example:

Amethyst: work on inner journeys or maybe you are being over emotional about something and need calming.

Raccoon: its meaning concerns thinking, mental difficulties and the stimulation of creativity.

Trees: need to be grounded- roots, reach for sacred knowledge- branches and leaves, no leaves-barren life, new shoots- new growth.

Always remember to look for your own meanings. Do not just settle on the referenced meaning if you feel it does not relate back to your own life. In any list of correspondences take note of the one(s) that stand out then reflect on the relevance to yourself.

If your symbols are animals you can visit a zoo, watch a video to find out its habits. Invite the animal to visit your dreams or welcome it into your Sacred Space and into your meditation.

How Do You Do It?

Go into your Sacred Space. Imagine the animal, flower, crystal, Deity etc in front of you. Open up your Chakras especially the heart, throat and third eye. Visualise spinning discs of energy over each chakra (can also picture individual colours or spinning rainbows). Listen with your whole self i.e. on physical, emotional, creative and soul levels. Connect with you other world messenger.

- What do you see?

- What colours stand out? On your messenger? On yourself?

- What thoughts come in?

- Are there any other people, things in your meditation?

- Listen for your messenger's voice?

- Ask any questions and remember to leave a silence for the answers.

When it is time to leave your Sacred Space, thank your messenger and allow yourself to slowly come into the now. Stretch into your body and open your eyes.

As soon as possible write down everything you remember. Lay it aside. When you return to this record later you can add anything else that comes to mind. Do not censor yourself.

****

As you have seen there are many ways to utilise meditation from simple relaxation to interpreting dreams, to connecting with your Spirit Guides. You can also explore past lives either by inviting the vision or by specific instructions. A good animal for Past Life work is crocodile as one of its meanings relates to past life issues.

Meditation is beneficial to health and spiritual well being. Regular use lowers stress levels but more importantly we can experience joy. Joy is an amazing emotion.

In many ways it is difficult to define as it is beyond happiness. In a channelled session connecting with Angels the massage came through **Joy just is.** For me it is bubbling energy tickling my insides and flooding my being and its colour is bright yellow. You may experience JOY in a different manner. Remember it is your JOY, not anyone else's joy.

MEDITATE AFFIRM BELIEVE FIND JOY

BE ALL YOU CAN BE

Ceremony and ritual used to be an integral part of life.

In tribal societies everyday life revolved around it. Stages of life were marked in a variety of ways: prayers, dance, sound (either, singing, vocal tones, drumming etc.) and special ceremonies. At dawn they welcomed the sun, before eating they gave thanks for food, and at the end of the day they welcomed the moon.

Shamans, medicine men and women, priestesses and elders devoted their lives connecting to Spirit and being the Guardians of the tribe's spiritual welfare.

However, all of the tribe connected to spirit through prayer and ritual in their daily life. When hunting prayers were offered up and gift's left as a means of honoring the animal's life and giving thanks to its soul or essence for the sustenance they were giving. Man hunted to live: for clothing, food and shelter. The entire animal was used.

Christianity changed this by placing ritual in the hands of one man and containing it in one place, to special days of the week and year and to set times. Tribal societies had special days and sacred places too, but ritual was carried out anywhere, anytime by anyone. People had a personal relationship with their God(s)/ Goddess (es) and with Spiritual practices.

For a long time families reserved Sundays for worship. Family prayers were said. Births, deaths and marriages were recorded in large family Bibles. Some religions still mark changes from birth to adulthood with special ceremonies: baptism, first communion, confirmation, Bar/Bat Mitzvahs, etc. Secularly we were given the key of the door or a gold watch, symbols to mark coming of age (originally 21 now 18) or retirement. Over time they lost their importance and became just another excuse for a party. Society still has a need for some ceremony and nowadays it is becoming common for celebrants to conduct naming ceremonies and offer services that were once the province of the clergy.

I feel that one side effect of disconnecting ourselves from spirit has been a loss of respect. We have lost respect for each other and for ourselves. This latter is the most important. If we cannot respect, honor and love ourselves we can only give lip service to other people and the planet.

We are one. We are all related. We are all energy.

Sometimes it is good to create a ritual around your meditations and/or affirmations. Lighting candles, burning oils, ringing bells or tolling brass bowls can set the tone for the meditation. Selecting a coloured candle or certain oils can support your affirmations as can choosing an appropriate day relevant to your affirmation.

Candles And Their Colours

Black	Strong banishings, bindings, limitations, loss, confusion, defining boundaries
Blue	Healing, wisdom, knowledge, dreams
Brown	Neutrality, stability, strength, grace, decision-making, pets, family
Gold	Masculinity, sun power, daylight hours, riches, the God
Green	Finances, security, employment, career, fertility, luck
Grey	Cancellations, anger, greed, envy
Light Blue	Calmness, tranquillity, patience, understanding, good health
Orange	Adaptability, zest for life, energy, imagination
Pink	Honour, friendships, virtue, morality, success, contentment, self-love, chastity, romance
Purple	Power, mild banishings, ambition, inner strength, divination
White	Purity, innocence, cleansings, childhood, truth, protection
Yellow	Communication, creativity, attraction, examinations, tests.

These colours can be related to: ribbons, threads, balloons, crayons, paints, glitter and anything else you may use to assist in meditations, spell castings, altars etc.

If you are cannot find a specific colour then you may use a white one, which can then be rubbed in oils or inscribed with symbols or words. Scott Cunningham's Incense, Oils and Brews is an excellent resource for oils and their correspondences. Runic symbols and Egyptian hieroglyphs can be used too. Of course you can also make up your own symbols. It cannot be said to often that it is the **intent** that counts.

Days Of Power

Monday	Day of the Moon, good for spellcraft that relates to the home, pets, family, feminine issues, psychic development and dreams
Tuesday	Mars rules this day, making it perfect for positive confrontation and being assertive. A day for business, work, getting your point across, courage and bravery
Wednesday	Mercury, the Winged Messenger rules this day, which is good for anything, connected to communication and creativity.
Thursday	This day is ruled by Jupiter and is good for money and prosperity spells as well as holiday and travel Magick.
Friday	Venus governs this day and all spells relating to love friends and socialising will be enhanced if performed on a Friday.
Saturday	Ruled by Saturn, this is a good day to perform magick concerning paying off debts or to call in money owing to you. Also for releasing negative and bad habits.
Sunday	The day of the Sun and anything connected to self-love and masculine issues will go well. This day is fabulous for 'ME' time.

You do not need to wait for a specific day of the week to carry out your meditation, spell work, manifestation, candle magick etc. If the need is now, do it now. The intent is more important. A specific day is just an added benefit.

Bibliography

Andrews, Ted **Animal Speak** Llewellyn Publications, St. Paul, Mn., USA

Conway, D.J. **Animal Magick** Llewellyn Publications, St. Paul, Mn., USA

Cunningham, Scott **The Complete Book of Incense, Oils & Brews** Llewellyn Publications, St.Paul, Mn., USA

Daxter, Brian & Carole **Reiki. A Gift of Love.** Inspirational Communications, Kalamunda, Western Australia

Dolfyn & Swimming Wolf **Shamanic Wisdom II.** Earthspirit, Inc. Oakland, CA. USA

Eason, Cassandra **Chakra Power.** Quantum, Slough, England.

Ellis, Richard **Reiki and The Seven Chakras.** Random House, London, England.

Gray, Miranda **Beasts of Albion.** Harper Collins , London, England.

King, Scott Alexander **Animal Messenger.** New Holland Publishers, Sydney, NSW, Australia.

Roderick, Timothy **The Once Unknown Familiar.** Llewellyn Publications, St. Paul, MN., USA.

Sams, Jamie & Carson, David **Medicine Cards.** St. Martins Press, New York. USA.

Wills, Pauline **Chakra Workbook.** Simon & Schuster, East Roseville, NSW, Australia.

Printed in the United States
By Bookmasters